short

long

hard

soft

How you can help

First Steps *sorting and opposites* introduces young children to the idea of opposites. Appealing photographs of children and everyday objects will help your child to learn words that describe relative sizes and positions.

 Enjoy talking about the photographs together. How many teddies can you see on the page? Are they the same or are they different?

 Encourage your child to compare the sizes of his* toys. Which is the biggest ball? Which is the smallest brick he can find?

There are lots of other ways you can help your child to learn about sorting and opposites. He could sort buttons or beads by colour, shape or size.

Use nursery rhymes like the Grand Old Duke of York or Jack Sprat to talk about opposites. It's fun to compare family members to find out who is the tallest, or who has the smallest feet.

**To avoid the clumsy 'he/she',
the child is referred to throughout as 'he'.*

Ladybird would like to thank Priscilla Hannaford, freelance editor on this series.

A catalogue record for this book is available
from the British Library

Published by Ladybird Books Ltd
A subsidiary of the Penguin Group
A Pearson Company
© LADYBIRD BOOKS LTD MCMXCVII

Photography on left hand page of
'shortest, tallest' spread © Julie Fisher MCMXCV

LADYBIRD and the device of a Ladybird are trademarks of
Ladybird Books Ltd Loughborough Leicestershire UK

sorting and opposites

by Lesley Clark

photography by Garie Hind

These socks are the *same*.

same

But these socks are *different*.

different

Are these slippers the same?

Are these slippers the same
or different?

Use practical everyday situations, such as tidying up, dressing and playing, to help your child explore things that are the **same** *and things that are* **different**.

Teddy bears, teddy bears –
just the same!

same

different

The elephant is *big*, but the mouse is *little*.

big

little

Look at your toys.

Are they all different sizes?

*Talk to your child about his own toys. Can he find one that's **big**? Can he find one that's **little**?*

The bear with the blue and yellow
bowl is *large*. The bear with the
yellow bowl is *middle-sized*.

large

middle-sized

The bear with the green bowl
is *small*.

small

These things are *cold*…

cold

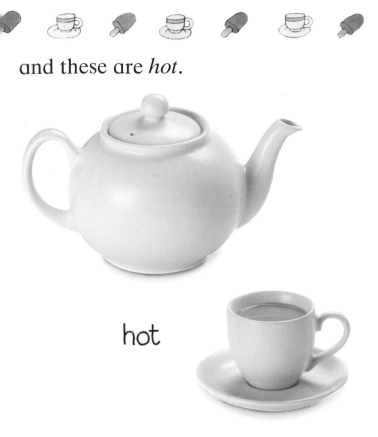

and these are *hot*.

hot

NEVER touch or go near hot things on your own.

Talking about these pictures of hot things will help your child to understand that they are dangerous and can hurt.

Jenny and her doll have their eyes open. They are *awake*.

awake

Jenny and her doll have their eyes shut. They are *asleep*.

asleep

This glass is *empty*.

empty

Fill it up with juice – now it's *full*!

full

Sally's bucket
is *heavy*!

heavy

Now her bucket
is *light*!

light

*Play water games at bath times, filling and emptying
lots of different sized containers.*

Look at the children, all in a row—
one, two, three, four.

Who is the *tallest*?

Who is the *shortest*?

shortest

tallest

Children love being measured. Keep a height chart in your child's bedroom as a visual reminder of how much he's grown.

Humpty is *fat*,
but the soldier is *thin*.

thin

fat

The beanbag is *soft* to sit on.

The rock is *hard*.

soft

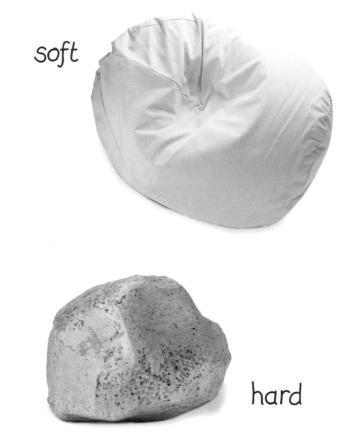

hard

Where would you rather sit?

One scarf is *short*.

long

The other is *long*.

short

Emma's hair is short, but Laura's hair is long.

short

long

Is your hair short or long?

*Look for other **long** and **short** things in the photograph. Emma has short sleeves, short socks, etc. Laura has long versions of the same things.*

Climb up to the *top* of the ladder...
one, two, three!

top

up

Whoosh... down to the *bottom*,
quick as can be!

down

bottom

Get *on* the bike...
one, two, three – go!

on

One, two, three – stop!
Now it's time to climb *off*.

off

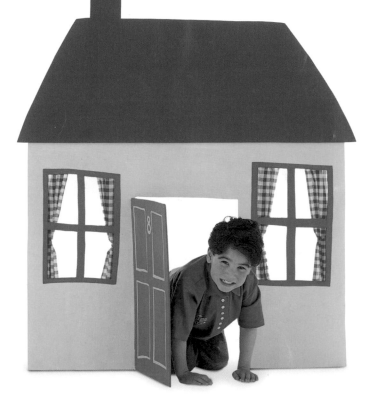

Open the door and say…

Hello!

open

Close the door, now it's time to go.

Goodbye!

closed

First Steps

Aimed at children aged 2 years and upwards, the **First Steps** range of mini hardback books, activity books and flash cards are designed to complement one another and can be used in any order.

mini hardbacks

- abc
- 123
- colours and shapes
- sorting and opposites
- time

Durable hardback books use photographs and illustrations to introduce important early learning concepts.

from **First Steps** *abc*